SUFFOLK SONNETS
AMONG OTHERS

SUFFOLK SONNETS
AMONG OTHERS

DAVID M V SPILLER

Copyright © 2024 David M V Spiller

The moral right of the author has been asserted.

Apart from any fair dealing for the purposes of research or private study, or criticism or review, as permitted under the Copyright, Designs and Patents Act 1988, this publication may only be reproduced, stored or transmitted, in any form or by any means, with the prior permission in writing of the publishers, or in the case of reprographic reproduction in accordance with the terms of licences issued by the Copyright Licensing Agency. Enquiries concerning reproduction outside those terms should be sent to the publishers.

Troubador Publishing Ltd
Unit E2 Airfield Business Park
Harrison Road, Market Harborough
Leicestershire LE16 7UL
Tel: 0116 279 2299
Email: books@troubador.co.uk
Web: www.troubador.co.uk

ISBN 978 1 805143 222

British Library Cataloguing in Publication Data.
A catalogue record for this book is available from the British Library.

Printed and bound in Great Britain by 4edge Limited
Typeset in 12.5pt Adobe Jenson Pro by Troubador Publishing Ltd, Leicester, UK

To my Darling wife, Gerry

Contents

Suffolk	1
Winter Storm on the Suffolk Coast	2
The Woodbridge Tide Mill	3
The Drummer Boys	4
Bawdsey Manor	5
Lunch on Aldeburgh Beach	6
Crabbing at Walberswick	7
Orford Castle	8
Walberswick	9
Pa Swimming at East Lane	10
Southwold	11
Fishing with Intent	12
Snape Maltings	13
The North Sea	14
The Aldeburgh Scallop	15
A Suffolk Childhood	16
Ramsholt	17
Shingle Street	18
Suffolk Skies	19
A Midsummer Sonnet	20
Longing for Summer	21
Cloudscapes	22
Tanning? A Warning!	23
Coronavirus - Covid 19	24
Orford Ness	25
Beware Feeding the Birds!	26
Pray to St Edmund	27
The Orford Merman	28

The River Deben	29
Sutton Hoo	30
Woodbridge	31
Thorpeness Meare	32
The Suffolk Punch	33
The Orwell Bridge	34
Global Warning	35
My Stalker	36
If Only…	37
Naked	38
A Sonnet for my Valentine	39
Democracy	40
Time	41
Some Reflections on Being Seventy	42
The Rock Pool	43
Sounds of Summer on a Beach	44
Christmas	45
On Writing a Sonnet	46
Finding Skye	47
Trees	48
Memories of Saxtead Green	49
The Old Cypriot Olive Tree	50
The Venus of Willendorf	51
January 30th, 1943	52
A Sound of Hornets	53
Thurlstone Rock, South Devon	54
The Warrior	55
Ad Astra Zeneca and Beyond!	56
Fishing for Mackerel with Old Jack	57
On Gazing Down to the Sea	58
The Holloway	59
Fledglings	60

The Sea	61
Schadenfreude	62
The Poppy	63
After my Heart Attack	64
In Memoriam	65
Seasons have their Day	66
Sunrise in the Woods	67
On Listening to the Song of a Robin	68
Our Garden	69
The Ancient Tree	70
Victoria Plums	71
The Mountains of the Western Isles	72
The Joy of Snow	73
A Merry Dance	74
The Byng Brook Bomb-Hole	75
Sleepless in Melton	76
Owning a Boat	77

Suffolk

Dear Suffolk lies upon the eastern coast,
first every day to greet the morning sun.
Of many favoured features it can boast
and quite unique is every single one.
Now, long ago the Suffolk Punch was raised
to pull the plough, grow the corn, our finest beast!
While Sutton Hoo a treasure highly praised
concealed the gold of Saxon kings deceased.
George Orwell, Constable and Gainsboro'
and Latitude for singers such as Ed,
Snape Maltings by the river in a meadow
with music such as Britten's it is led.
A peaceful, gentle county in the sun
the perfect place to live for anyone!

Winter Storm on the Suffolk Coast

We struggled on the shingle 'gainst the wind.
The ice cold blast came screaming from the north.
The sea looked like an iron land, unkind.
 Our faces, cut by spray as we set forth.
Thick coats we wore felt threadbare in this blast.
We heard the seabirds overhead drear cries,
impale the lowering clouds which were so vast.
As sun was setting through our shielded eyes
The tide rose high and milled the stones like grain.
The northern sea a-churning with the haze,
just like a tango dressed in driving rain.
We never would forget those freezing days.
For we mere mortals like to take control,
such wintry storms excite our human soul.

The Woodbridge Tide Mill

The Mill has stood here for *eight hundred years;
most famous icon of this market town.
'Twas owned by Augustinian Friars,
before *King Henry took it for his own.
From Good Queen Bess, the canny Seckford bought it,
and over time it fell to disrepair.
But then the folk of Woodbridge town caught it,
to make of it a working mill with care.
 Now at peace, a very famous image,
and photographed for calendars and such;
drawn and painted in an arty scrimmage;
it has been done, one could say, far too much!
But it is something that we truly love,
And better yet when filmed by drones above?

* The original Tide Mill was built some time before 1170. King Henry Vlll confiscated it during the Dissolution of the Monasteries.

The Drummer Boys

Two boys are left to call the troops to fight,
the bugler fell but isn't one to moan.
The drummer plays the beat with all his might,
he will not cease although he drums alone.
The battle rages on, in heat and dust.
The enemy are weakened, on the run,
the victory is ours, in God we trust.
beneath the unforgiving Afghan sun.
So many lives were lost in far off lands
where British rulers' laws and God held sway,
but now, no longer resting in our hands.
Ideas of Empire have been swept away.
For earth's proud empires always end in tears
But memories will linger on for years.

Bawdsey Manor

The fabled towers display across their land,
they gaze far out to sea with righteous ease.
Yet hidden bunkers lay beneath the sand
guarded by some ancient groves of trees.
This house was built by *Quilter to display
success and wealth for all the world to see.
But then came war and with it disarray;
So radar was researched behind the lea.
The Nazis did not know of this new power,
the RAF developed it alone.
At Bawdsey 'twas the manor's finest hour,
thanks to the man who'd sold his telephones.
And now the house is smiling in the sun
and hosts young students there for summer fun.

* Sir Cuthbert Quilter made his fortune in the 1890s manufacturing telephones.

Lunch on Aldeburgh Beach

The queue winds through the door and people smile;
a pungent smell pervades the seaside air.
For fish and chips the wait is all worthwhile,
and patient folk can only stand and stare.
Their feast they will consume upon the strand,
or on the wall where greedy seagulls screech.
For this the best meal in our ancient land,
our dining room the sloping pebble beach.
We are an island race and love our fish,
we fry it in hot oil all dressed in batter,
with vinegar and salt as some might wish,
to eat with hands, knives and forks don't matter!
It's 'haute cusine' while eating with your fingers
yet knowing that the scent quite often lingers.

Crabbing at Walberswick

We stare down to the water far below
to seek our prey just lurking out of sight.
We lower baited lines, no need to throw
and try to not disturb or cause a fright.
And then we see the crab has just latched on.
The biggest one you ever, ever saw!
It gripped the bacon morsel with aplomb
and dangled there with pincers to the fore.
But then the line went suddenly quite slack,
Our quarry fell to freedom with a splash!
Now we would never have to put it back,
'cos he had simply vanished in a flash.
Just like our lives our fortunes ebb and flow.
And for this crab it was now time to go.
For he'd been caught a hundred times or more
but never keeps a tally of the score!

Orford Castle

By Orford Town there stands a mighty keep.
Good King Henry had it built of stone,
with dungeons dug beneath, so very deep,
where luckless men were chained in dark alone.
The keep was built to crush *The Anarchy,
when nobles were refusing to obey,
which did not please the lordly monarchy,
who roughed them up and sent them on their way.
The castle stands, thanks to benefactors,
and tourists come to watch a joust or plays,
and merry costumed folk, 're-enactors',
who just for fun relive the 'good ole days'.
For some do hanker to go back in time,
but not for long, there's too much muck and grime!

Henry ll (1154–1189)

The Anarchy (1135–1189) was a rebellion by certain nobles over the succession.

Walberswick

A quiet enclave 'pon the suffolk coast
lies Walberswick serene amongst the dunes.
Of many famous artists it can boast,
who've painted and composed such clever tunes.
It has a peaceful charm for all to see,
no gaudy funfair here, no noisy crowds,
where city dwellers always love to flee
in hopes of sunny skies and pretty clouds.
By many it's a place to be enjoyed,
with lots of names familiar, some quite posh.
There's Coldstream, Dunstan and of course a Freud,
and don't forget young Rennie Mackintosh.
The beach at Walberswick is one fine strand,
in rain or shine the fairest in the land.

Pa Swimming at East Lane

He'd dance around behind his towel to strip
to put his swimming shorts on, being shy.
Since winter he'd have waited for this trip
now sun shone bright amid the azure sky.
He hobbled down on pebbles t'wards the edge
and walked these stones which brought such awful pain.
For he was drawn and balanced on a ledge
and knew he's right to come here, to East Lane.
My father used to swim here all alone,
to seek some peace and quiet solitude.
He'd fought a war now wanted to atone.
I think a swim helped him to feel renewed.
We'll never know what thoughts went though his head
and sadly never shall, for he's long dead.

Squadron Leader J. L.Spiller DFC 1913–1986
RAF Bomber Command 1939–1945

Southwold

The town of Southwold rests beside the Blythe,
a pleasant place with ancient pedigree.
St Edmund's church where once they paid the tithe.
There's famous Adnam's much loved brewery.
In times gone by it was a fishing port,
men used to fish for herring, cod and sprats,
but times have changed and trippers now are sought
for holdays and renting out nice flats.
It hosts a lighthouse and's near Latitude,
the Swan Hotel, pier, sundry shops and bars.
In summer time they welcome multitudes
of visitors and trippers and some 'stars',
with many second homes let out for rent
now that is something locals might resent.

Fishing with Intent

Along the shore, in rain, with switched off phone,
you see him sitting in his one-man tent,
which from afar looks like a standing stone,
is catching lots of fish his 'sole' intent?
Coarse fishing is his game and his retreat,
from noisy work, noisy kids, noisy wife.
A busy worker always on his feet
and this his solace, rest from busy life.
He has his rods, some lunch and fresh dug bait,
new jig-hooks, fleece-lined coat and hat and gloves,
with arctic boots and thus prepared to wait.
For this is what he does and what he loves.
To catch a fish? He really doesn't care,
he only wants some peace in good sea air.

Snape Maltings

Among those sighing reeds the Maltings stand,
a place for song and music and creative arts.
On hallowed ground encircled by marsh land
and now securely held in all our hearts.
Opened by the Queen in sixty seven,
twice burnt down and twice it was restored.
With shops and galleries,a perfect heaven,
for retail therapy 'tis much adored.
It hosts the festival for nearby Aldeburgh,
founded by Britten (Ben) and Peter Pears.
They wrote and played, sang throughout the borough,
with dramas, laughter, action and some tears.
And now it is a place of world renown
a special place which also wears a *crown.

* The Crown Pub, Snape.

The North Sea

Scion of the great atlantic ocean,
formed when ancient ice began to melt
As Albion established this our nation
Defensive waters circled like a belt.
A shallow sea and it's so good for fishing,
Famous for its storms and deadly squalls.
Causing tragedies as men go missing,
cyclonic winds can make such dreadful falls.
The North Sea has inspired and artists smitten,
as Turner's painting seas and storms that raged.
And music from the likes of Pears and Britten
and paintings from the famous *Golden Age.
For we should be in awe of nature's might.
If we abuse it we are due a fright!

* The Golden Age refers to the Dutch Golden Age, of Dutch artists like Van der Velde and Bakhuisen *et al*. Not forgetting Rembrandt and Vermeer.

The Aldeburgh Scallop

Along the strand just north of Aldeburgh town
a contraversial sculpture rules the beach.
"I hear those voices that will not be drowned!"
cut through its husk, as hov'ring seagulls screech.
Made of English steel, so many folk are smitten,
The giant shells arranged for all to see.
It is of course erected for Ben Britten,
and will stand there for all eternity?
Some think it's perfection a work of art,
others not so and they want it destroyed.
It must be cut down now, dragged off in a cart.
Those who admire it, they've always approved.
Others think the sculpture spoils a lovely view.
Well what do you think? And what would you do?

A Suffolk Childhood

Playing in the meadows by the river
during endless days of summer larks,
always come to mind just like a sliver
of brightest light which lightens up the dark.
Clambering on rocks down by the seashore,
running through the uncut field of hay.
A plaster on your knee, which once was sore.
Watching hawks a-hunting for their prey.
Growing up in Suffolk, all so long ago,
running free in fields or on the beach,
a time of simple games perhaps in snow,
memories now fading out of reach.
For we are growing older as we must
and one day in the future will be dust.

Ramsholt

We love to go down to the Ramsholt Arms,
close by the Deben, down a sandy hill.
A peaceful haven, one of Suffolk's charms
where you can meet or eat and drink your fill.
Above the bank the ancient church held sway.
It's been there for about a thousand years.
A lonely tower, with hamlet swept away,
which caused the locals many bitter tears.
Now tourists come to walk the river path,
as children play along the sandy shore,
and sailors come for mooring up their crafts.
A quiet place to rest for rich and poor.
Beneath this peaceful calm there still remains,
echoes of war, bravery,death and pain.

A flying fortress ditched in the River Deben on 20th Feb 1945,
Eight of the USA crew perished, two survived.
There is a memorial plaque by the door to the Ramsholt Arms.

Shingle Street

We settle on some shingle, drop our things,
and stare across the water's ruffled waves.
We slip off clothes then 'costumes' shyly cling.
We know to swim we must be truly brave.
So stumble on wet pebbles down the slope,
arriving at the water's edge too soon.
We mutter words like "Freezing!" as we hope,
maybe we'd change our minds, this afternoon?
But no! We wade in to the murky sea,
and quickly dive into the icey foam,
and surface gasping needing strong hot tea!
And being warm again when back at home.
For swimming at the "Street" seems loads of fun,
but really never, ever should be done!!

Suffolk Skies

When I am far away and think of home,
the skies of Suffolk always come to mind.
An endless blue above some briney foam
or lowering clouds brought on a gentle wind.
An early dawn arising though dark trees,
or evening shadows creeping over lawns,
or storm down-river meeting angry seas.
These are the things for which my tired eyes yearn.
Artists try to capture these enchantments,
in music, words or paints or even ink.
They've no use for any false enhancements,
and free to work in any way they think.
For wonders Suffolk surely has no dearth,
in truth it is a piece of Heaven on earth.

A Midsummer Sonnet

Midsummer day brings thoughts of cold winters,
days will grow shorter as earth spins away!
Soon will the snow and icicles' splinters
sparkle and glitter in frozen array.
A few weeks ago were the days when we wandered
warm by the seashore and riverside banks.
We'd pick up the flotsam like treasure we'd plundered,
finding a "jewel" and murmuring *"Thanks!"
And cozy by fires we'll wait for the spring,
get used to the changes, live in the dark.
We'll wait for warm days to make our hearts sing!
Gaze into blue skies, smile up to the lark.
All seasons return as day follows night
and poets will want sweet sonnets to write.

* We regularly go beachcombing, clearing up plastic etc. Some of the finds are recycled creatively.

Longing for Summer

We longed for the summer when we would be free,
and never could wait for schoolwork to end.
We'd run to the beach and down to the sea,
with hopes for warm days and playing with friends.
We'd seek out the places where we could swim
in rivers so gently that flowed 'neath low trees.
And finding flat stones to throw and to skim,
then lie in the sun drying off in the breeze.
When nights are so short and full moon so bright
and stars in their thousands lit up the sky.
We'd steal through the meadows like wraiths in the night,
as barn owl glides over with silken sigh.
When summer time's done, and ending with rain
leaving that small quiet dull ache of pain.

Cloudscapes

On windy days I watch as clouds go by,
they block the sun and roll across their stage.
Like castle towers, canyons in the sky?
Or shifting shapes portray a hint of rage?
On sunny days dear fluffy sheep will graze,
and strange enough they have no need for legs.
For quite by chance emerging from the haze,
now they are chickens sitting on some eggs.
And yet again those changes never last,
as rain arrives and with it thund'rous noise!
And angry waves crash down with noisy blast.
Now lightening's flash portrays the scene so poised.
But just like humans, they are in the mood,
well, they'll appear to be extremely rude!

Tanning? A Warning!

We love to bask and soak up all the sun,
we have to get tanning for bronze or gold.
For us it seems just like some harmless fun,
and never mind it makes our skin grow old.
We travel far and swim in turquoise seas,
and lie on sand and frolic in the foam,
we seek a change of hue while at our ease,
so we can flaunt ourselves when we get home.
We know the dangers that this tan can bring,
and cover up with hats and factored 'Creme'
we never spend too long on sunny swing,
for danger lurks in ev'ry bright sunbeam.
We have to change to bronzed perfection, right?
But trouble looms, and we will look a sight!

Coronavirus - Covid 19

A nasty virus came from far away,
invisible and deadly, quite unknown.
Too quick, it stole so many souls each day,
some slipped into the darkness quite alone.
The politicians asked for calm at first.
"Please wash your hands and keep yourselves at home!"
As then the masses had to be coerced,
with folk denied to meet with friends or roam.
*Hundreds now are dying every day,
as medics work so hard for this to cease.
Some others will distract with pithy play
as people watch and hope for some release.
For we are hapless mortals who must wait
to meet our future and confront our fate.

* Written at the height of the pandemic.

Orford Ness

From on the Orford Quay you catch a boat
across the tidal river to the Ness.
A quiet refuge and a bit remote.
It looks quite ruined and a spooky mess.
Buildings are damaged and seem somewhat strange,
a pagoda and bunker for rockets?
'Twas a place for testing a new bomb's range,
and beacons for radar with sprockets.
Now we're at peace so nature can heal it,
and aerodynamics are just for the birds,
terns and cormorants, gulls and the peewits,
some writers now praise it with beautiful words.
The work led to vict'ry in both world wars
let's hope all is settled with no more old scores.

Beware Feeding the Birds!

So come to Aldeburgh buy your fish and chips!
But be aware don't feed the gulls that swoop,
and know they try to snatch fish from your lips,
or even worse deliver bombs of 'poop'!
The penalty for feeding greedy pests
is 'blazoned everywhere and clearly signed.
You too will be considered for arrest,
for certain, without doubt you will be fined.
While seagulls make a very pretty sight,
they're lazy birds who want an easy meal.
For fish and chips they don't care who they fight!
With tourists they've no shame so they just steal.
Beware! Your food will have an extra cost,
if to the seagull's beak it has been 'lost'.

Pray to St Edmund

Edmund the saint of pandemics and kings,
crowned king of Angles when only a lad.
A good man and holy, slain by Vikings,
a martyr for Jesus, he died, which was sad.
Tied to a stake and murdered with arrows,
his head was cut off and thrown into woods.
The Suffolk folk wept so full of sorrows
and prayed for him, heads bowed under their hoods.
Came forth a wolf and who watched his remains.
A poor boy was saved made no longer blind.
Edmund was sainted thus banished were Danes
and pilgrims come his golden tomb to find.
Now in our time of this deadly virus
Pray to St Edmund for him to save us!

The Orford Merman

A long time ago in old Orford town,
some men went out fishin' with such high hopes.
Their wives they did weep a-feared they would drown,
as the sailors set off and tightened their ropes.
But they'd never 've guessed what came to pass,
"Now haul in them nets!" cried the old helmsman.
But it wasn't herring, sole nor bass.
"Twas a slimey, frightenin', real Merman!
They were scared when they showed it to their kin,
so 'twas hung in the castle by its tail.
They took it to church to confess its sin,
yet it never spoke but only would wail.
While they were deciding to do what was right,
the merman swam off right into the night!

The River Deben

The timeless river winds through marsh and lea,
'twas much attacked by Vikings on their raids.
It made a perfect 'road' in from the sea
and later when peace reigned it ferried trades.
But now it's home for many trippers' yachts,
each summer they return to have some fun.
They come in droves, in fact there's lots snd lots!
While on the *'wall' the folk in lycra run.
The river does not change as all else might.
Coralled by landscape and an earthen wall,
'twas built the high tides and their floods to fight.
Now if it fails then we would lose it all.
And wooden wrecks which die upon the mud
are just as frail as human flesh and blood.

* The embankment that prevents the river flooding.

Sutton Hoo

Who-ever was buried at Sutton Hoo?
We don't really know. Do you think you do?
"Let's see what's in those mounds!", I say.
Said Mrs.Pretty on one fine day.
So Basil the gardener set off with his spade
and found such treasure as a king had made.
Most say it was Raedwold, a brave Saxon King
who was interred with treasures and everything.
There were buckles and swords, jewels galore
and dig as they did, they found more and more!
It all brought about so much consternation,
that dear Mrs Pretty gave it all to the nation.
And now it's displayed in the British Museum
and not left to rot in a ship's mausoleum.

Woodbridge

Woodbridge is a charming place to be,
there's always someone busking with guitar,
a market town well-steeped in history,
a pleasant place to spend a happy hour.
The coffee shops, the delis and the clothes,
the pubs and restaurants, Indian and Chinese,
they all combine to make,well, goodness knows,
the perfect town to visit at your ease.
The river Deben flows beside the town
where once so many boats did ply their trade.
For muddy banks and tides it is well known,
where once the Vikings pillaged and did raid.
It is a place for all and hosts so many types,
to look just like a local, best wear stripes!

Thorpeness Meare

For a day of wonder out in a boat
you need go no further than on to the Meare
To go it's just great for ventures afloat
in a place which so many hold so dear.
Visit a castle and row yourself there!
See the old crocodile's jaws open wide.
Take out a kayak,whatever you dare!
Peggotty's house is a good spot to hide.
A beautiful place with islands and more.
The water's not deep with ducks and some swans,
you'll love it so much and might go ashore.
A great place for kids, a Suffolk icon.
With the "house in the clouds" floating above
It's a place to enjoy, which everyone loves.

The Suffolk Punch

His muscled neck and shining *chesnut red
of celebrated Suffolk Punch or *"Sorrel"
are noted traits of this fine horse, well bred.
A gentle one as rare as the red squirrel.
Of shorter build than Clydesdale or the Shire
they're known for hauling ploughs and heavy carts.
As Munnings' famous works lit golden fire
in paint or sculpture they inspire such art.
The breed is now in danger and so few,
no longer workers and their tasks are done.
To protect them now is what we must do.
They've earned their days in the glorious sun.
They're special and rare like finest gold dust,
so please do support the Suffolk Punch Trust.

* The traditional spelling, leaving out the 't' is used when describing the Suffolk Punch. Also known as the Suffolk Sorrel.

The Orwell Bridge

Its mighty pillars stride across the vale
to link two river banks with Ipswich Town.
By master builders it was built so well,
it's hailed by all and famed with such renown.
It shortens journeys by so many hours,
to speed the goods we get from *Felixstowe.
A transport hub for cars and even flowers
from overseas or any place you go.
But there's a complication in a high wind,
which was considered when it was proposed,
but we are used to it and then we find,
that in a gale the bridge is always closed.
As safety first is ever to the fore
when crossing a high bridge from shore to shore.

* The port of Felixstowe is the UK's largest container port

Global Warning

Pollution is the price we pay for progress,
we cannot drive a car without *exhaust.
We have to stop just adding to this mess
or else we'll face another Holocaust.
For everything we want there is a price,
the gods of old were well aware of that!
The sea devours our coastline in a trice
and rising tides will gobble just like rats.
We still insist on burning fossil fuels,
we *have* to fly and never mind the cost.
We act just like those silly thoughtless fools
who spoil it all with litter they have tossed.
If we continue ruining this world,
then into darkness we will all be hurled.

* The manufacture of batteries for electric cars still produces CO_2, but they are working on it!

My Stalker

You slip into my vision like a sea,
in waves of diamonds and of broken glass
you conjure with my equanimity,
then I can only yield until you pass.
You come for reasons quite unknown to me,
perhaps by coffee, choc'late or some stress?
The pills I take compound the alchemy,
I give myself to Triptan's sweet caress.
At last when you begin to fade away,
I'm left exhausted and in truth bereft.
You waste my time and really spoil the day,
my spark is gone, a headache's all that's left.
When all is said and done, you are a pain,
my useless, pointless stalker, my migraine.

If Only...

If humankind had never walked on earth
and never farmed the land or cut down trees,
if only animals had given birth
and only fish and birds had crossed the seas.
If only man had not made vicious wars
nor awful weapons that annihilate
nor baseless pride that settles ancient scores,
for man should only love and never hate.
The humans are the only problem here,
they smash and leave their rubbish all around,
now that is killing all that is so dear
and all that we have left is poisoned ground.
Our planet has been warmed, is it too late?
The tipping point draws nearer to our fate.

Naked

When summer comes I must beg your pardon
some folk will think I'm really rather rude.
I like to go out to our lovely garden
take off my clothes and sunbathe in the nude!
It may seem odd or even quite deluded,
but rest assured I'm sane and not a creep,
my special place is really quite secluded
to lie in sunny shade and go to sleep.
To walk as Adam, when completely naked
especially on summer's sunny days
the walm air calms and feels so very sacred
private, alone, without another's gaze.
For came we to this world unique and rare,
no clothes, no covers and completely bare!

A Sonnet for my Valentine

Together we have been for many years
Eyes met when sitting on a classroom desk
we used to go to pubs and drink some beers
and teachers talked about the picturesque.
My place at art school happened just by chance
someone had left so I could be there too.
We kissed and often we would freely dance,
It was a stroke of luck that I met you.
You gave true love, to me a thing so rare.
Now we have lived and loved in wedded bliss,
it is so sweet a thing to taste and care
my dear love, for you, so seal it with a kiss.
We know not what the fates may have in store,
but what we have will last for ever more.

Democracy

In an autocratic country
where people are imprisoned if they dare
to call for justice and a fairer vote
and they all find a system so unfair,
if they should try to rock their nation's boat.
One candidate is set for you to "choose".
The Party *knows* what's right and what is wrong.
So vote for him for he shall never lose.
They have it written in their national song;
the people "reign" supreme in their fair land.
Their leader says, and he has all the power.
He wants us all to know that all is planned.
We're in our place and he's up in his tower
and he makes sure that all dissent is void
like insects on the ground it is destroyed.

Time

We cannot see nor touch this thing called time,
we cannot hear nor smell it, there's no taste,
'tis ever present, you can hear the chime,
yet it is something we should never waste.
We fashion clocks to mark its passing by,
so we can measure it and check its speed.
And sighing 'tempus fugit', time does fly!
But still it marches on, as Time decrees.
it stands not still, for no-one will it wait,
to gain advantage or to catch a bus.
It shows no mercy when you're running late
no use is there in making any fuss.
Without it there could never truly be,
our earth, our sky, nor even you and me!

Some Reflections on Being Seventy

Now I've been here for three score years and ten
and life has lead me through so many days.
I've seen what damage men can do to men
yet being good and kind are the best ways.
We struggle to achieve our precious goals
and hope that all will turn out for the best
but then our 'ship' is sometimes full of holes
and sinks down in the deep to darkest rest.
The most important thing for me is love,
to have and hold and be in such a place
as warrants everything from up above,
the sun ,the rain, the wind upon my face.
Such things affirm our fragile life down here
before we have to leave this special sphere.

The Rock Pool

We clustered round the pool between the rocks
our feet a ghostly white in watery shade,
as scattered near lay useless shoes and socks.
Now when we walked the weeds all gently swayed,
the surface of the water was like glass.
I moved my net around this magic place,
so clear and crystal when I made the pass,
and caught a shrimp with shock upon its face.
I didn't know exactly what was best,
it seemed to me so frightened it would die,
I didn't want to let its end distress,
so put it back and watched as it did fly.
The animals that lurk in all these pools
survive, so prove *they* are not silly fools!

Sounds of Summer on a Beach

Eyes closed on summer days of long ago,
when I lay dozing on a sandy beach.
I heard the crying child who'd stubbed his toe
and distant calls of seabirds' noisy screech.
A choking outboard spluttered far away,
some children wanting pushing on the swing,
the gentle lapping waves across the bay,
and Radio One as someone tries to 'sing'.
The barking dog that only wants its ball,
the hawker calling out his gaudy wares,
a girl dropped her ice cream and lost it all.
An old man hears his dying pals and stares…
This day will pass and will be photographed.
Could we forget the copper when he laughed?

Christmas

Soon is the mystery of Christmas time,
for most we hold that day so very dear.
Is it the tinkle of a bell that chimes,
or pretty lighting at this time of year?
The story of a birth of one foretold,
who came to save us from our human ways
of hate and selfishness and the fools' gold
of shallow fame and social media praise?
A child was born with nothing, on some hay
to show us how to lead a better life.
To think of others every single day
and not to agitate in needless strife.
For we are blest if we all care and love
for world, for seas, for earth and air above.

On Writing a Sonnet

I'm going to write a sonnet of mine
and follow the rules of ancient rubric,
to keep to ten syllables in every line
with always pentametres iambic.
Fourteen lines one's permitted to write
to stick to the good old Shakespeare form
it doesn't seem much, in fact rather tight,
but it's what's demanded and is the norm.
This format I've chosen is not hard
It's a structure that has so very few rules!
'Twas the favourite of the dear old bard,
it's always been taught in all the best schools.
These laws of the sonnet are there for all
and Will wrote several as I recall.

Finding Skye

They had a dream to travel way up north
to find the peace that they had so longed for,
they sought the perfect place so they set forth
to seek a home with views of hills and shore.
Despite some setbacks and the hand of fate,
they found a little croft complete with thatch,
they made their plans and set the parting date,
then sallied forth to finalise their catch.
Through rain and snow they drove to find their home,
and on the island found where it did lie,
a fabled place where heroes once did roam,
the bonny prince's refuge, Isle of Skye.
They've had to fight for every single thing,
and now can live just like a queen and king.

Trees

So many trees once grew across the land,
the oak,the ash, the elm, the beech, the pine,
to make the things we needed cut by hand
for houses, ships and wagons, rough or fine.
Then forest land was cleared to plant the corn
and sheep and cows could gently chew the cud.
The trees were felled and woods were left forlorn
when war and fighting churned so much to mud.
We must preserve our woodlands and our leas
to help produce a cleaner atmosphere
to purify the air and give us lease
from here on earth, up to the stratosphere.
For we depend on trees for every breath
without them we are lost. There's only death!

Memories of Saxtead Green

Memories of Saxtead, long summer day,
watch them run grasses right up to their knees,
cloudy gold pollen, amid uncut hay,
 butterfly chasing, avoiding the bees.
Tinkling of laughter and what will they reap?
Our youngest lions, cheering and tumbling,
all unaware as an old lion *sleeps.
Thunderclouds gather, hear the loud rumbling,
children so young as their old Grandpa lingers.
The †sails overhead have not moved for years.
Breaking the daisy chain hung through their fingers,
end of the day, more laughter and tears.
Our life an instant of sacred wonder,
like flash of lightning in summer thunder.

* My father in the nursing home
† Sails of Saxtead mill

The Old Cypriot Olive Tree

I've stood here for more than a thousand years,
and watched as the invaders came and went,
Egyptians, Persians, and Greek buccaneers,
some apostles like Paul and Mark were sent.
Arabs were followed by Richard the first,
here married his queen Berengaria.
As I was growing the island was cursed
by the Ottomans, even scarier!
Then the British arrived and civil war
divided with fighting quite serious.
The Turks once again were a bit of a bore
as they battled 'gainst Bishop Makarios.
Yet all of this time I've stood in this soil,
producing an ocean of olive oil.

The Venus of Willendorf

You stand mute with face so very concealed,
your breasts hanging down so full and so fair,
your arms are held back and belly revealed,
your myst'ry adorns, no secrets you share.
Below your navel your sex is quite neat,
beneath, your thighs with your knees clamped so tight,
ankles are hidden and so are your feet
of your purpose you shed so little light.
Like Venus that hangs in the infinite dark,
you are so motionless never to move.
A Goddess perhaps the seasons to mark?
A lady who came from the earth to love?
Your people are gone, now you're left alone
a queen of the harvest without her throne.

January 30th, 1943

All standing in line one cold afternoon
the crew of the bomber stares back at me.
All is now ready to fly by the moon.
Are they now thinking of their destiny?
The man in the middle, my father, looks grey,
but what are his thoughts ? He'll fly to Berlin !
The black and white shot gives nothing away.
They wait and know that there'll be such a din.
He wasn't shot down and lived to be free !
He tried to forget what went in his war,
it affected him greatly, but could never release
himself from horror which he did so abhor.
Sadly I never knew my father well,
I think that he had been through too much hell.

A Sound of Hornets

The sound of hornets cut the morning light,
as saws sliced up the single chestnut tree.
I watched as men in helmets dressed to fight
snuffed out the *'candles' so beloved of bee.
It gave a favourite perch to hunting owl,
who silent swooped above the drying hay.
It heard the barking vixen make its howl
when dark came down to end a sunny day.
They want to build big houses now instead,
with drive and double garage and a lawn,
integral kitchen and neat flower bed,
the creatures that lived here have now all gone.
But who are we to stop these changes here
because we held our status quo so dear?

* Chestnut tree's candles

Thurlestone Rock, South Devon

Astride the shore the mighty portal stands,
since ancient times it's overlooked the beach.
Its grandeur gazes down upon the sands,
while seabirds swoop above and loudly screech.
A vast two-legged beast it never moves,
a guardian rock that oversees our shores
and winding coastal paths, high cliffs and coves.
It has no need of bloodied teeth and claws
against the tides and ocean's fiercest waves.
Against the thief who wants to rob and maim,
against those fiends who want us to enslave.
All will be dealt with just the very same,
with silent stare and bored indifference,
just like a rock and not a wooden fence.

The Warrior

This warrior has fought a thousand times,
in many far off lands across the seas.
He's known so many different climes
and cooled himself in ev'ry welcome breeze.
He's killed so many hard and valiant men,
but always swore allegiance to his lord.
He's battled on the hills and down the glen.
He's lived his life completely by the sword.
He never talked of kin or gave a name,
known simply as 'The Warrior' was he.
He never fought for gold or shallow fame,
but only took the prize of victory.
Now he is dead and on his deathbed lies,
in sand and dust and visited by flies.

Ad Astra Zeneca and Beyond!

We walked through town to queue up for our jabs,
like hundreds more are doing every day.
We kept our fingers crossed and hoped the labs
had got it right and 'safe' as they would say.
We calmly queued then showed our special code,
and answered questions, "Can you taste and smell?"
"Have you any symptoms that have just showed?"
"No." I said, "I'm fine, feeling very well."
The needle flashed and plunged into my arm,
I felt a tiny sting like from a gnat,
and that was all 'twas over, all was calm.
I rolled my sleeve down knowing that was that.
We walked home feeling safer, then until,
later on we both felt, er rather ill!

Fishing for Mackerel with Old Jack

Under low clouds in a watery light
we set off to fish for the silvered ones.
We took lines of feathers, hoping they'd bite,
and prayed we'd have successful runs.
When three miles out we thought we'd try
so drifted on tides and let our lines out.
We hauled back and forth and soon fish did fly
right into the boat as we gave each a clout.
Then out of the blue my line went so taught,
I yelled "It's a big one!" and hauled in the mass,
as they fell round my feet, a whole shoal I'd caught.
It wasn't the mackerel but golden sea bass!
*A snap of a boy with sun in his eyes,
Jack keeps on display, as I hold up my prize.

* Many years later, Old Jack still had a photo of me on his TV holding up strings of mackerel.

On Gazing Down at the Sea

We sit around and watch the setting sun,
as daylight fades across the dusty hills.
We see the homeward bound, their work now done,
as creeping breezes gently bring dark chills.
The distant sea lies dormant in its bay,
the life that it supports in restless sleep.
The changing moon is never here to stay,
as fisher-folk haul bounty from the deep.
This island has been safe at many times
for passing souls who built, then called it home.
They mined the ore, with no more wish to roam.
For we're now here where ancients used to be
two thousand years ago, still staring at the sea.

The Holloway

We wander down the gently sloping way
worn out of earth by countless flocks snd feet,
by which some came to sing to dance or pray
or tell their news or simply just to meet?
The ancient oaks now gaze upon this track
where children play when hiding to amuse.
Some rest beside them when they travel back
so trees have seen and heard their urgent news.
These earthly banks are worn away by use,
and thus reveal the underlying clay.
from which we're made and then we are set loose
to care for it or see it washed away.
And does this hollow way which we have seen
tell us of when He walked on pastures green?

Fledglings

Today the sparrows finally have fledged,
their parents still care all day for their brood,
which enjoys to hop on top of the hedge,
and demanding juicy morsels of food.
They flutter their wings to gain their reward
their twittering tinkles like shattering glass.
Their dutiful parents finds it quite hard
but all of their efforts are really first class.
In a few days they'll have mastered the knack
of feeding themselves with insects or seeds.
Then they will fly off and never come back.
They are clever and gifted and brave indeed!
These wonders of nature are ours to see
and need to be treasured by you and me.

The Sea

The waves explode upon the shingle shore,
and crash just like an off-piste avalanche,
with seabirds caterwauling as they soar
as rain drives down in patterns for a dance.
Our restless ocean's soul is so inconstant
her fickle ways can comfort or dismay
but her mood can alter in an instant
and seems to do so every single day.
So happy when she's gentle and so calm,
despondent when she's piqued and volatile.
I hope that I shall never come to harm
in gale force winds or lightning storms so vile.
An island race surrounded by the sea,
this truly *sceptered isle's so fine and free

* Apologies to WS!

Schadenfreude

My painting's shown beside more than a few,
the summer show's array where many hang.
The sculptures and the works of brightest hue.
But then at home that night my mobile rang.
The gallery has pleasing news, they're glad,
they called to tell me that my painting's sold.
I'm pleased at first but then a little sad.
I liked it but to lose it leaves me cold.
In every work I do there's part of me,
it's such that I have spent to fabricate,
my painting of a rough and restless sea,
a journey which my brush did navigate.
Those feelings for a sale which were so bleak,
now I'm upset when nothing sells this week!

The Poppy

The poppy is a sweet and gentle thing,
on summer days they billow in the breeze,
They skip among the fields as if to sing
and decorate the paths and down the leas.
Their blooms are red as blood which gives us life,
their petals soft as silk from far off lands.
Their symbol is a peace with no more strife,
as children hold them gently in their hands.
Their eyes are dark as on a secret face,
so full of mystery and ancient ways.
The †god of sleep who lingers in their place,
sends dreams to us, so nights are changed to days.
The poppy blooms but only once a year,
we wait… it will return… so have no fear!

* Morpheus, god of sleep, hence morphine
† And in dreams where things change shape or morph

After my Heart Attack

Last Thursday I was fitted with a stent
by doctors with a very special skill.
Unblocking arteries is their intent
so cleared the lipid pools that made me ill.
Remote control, an X-ray guided tube,
delivered to the spot with gentle stealth,
a small balloon expanded precious mesh
and brought me back the chance of better health.
For nursing staff are such a noble breed,
they help all fellow humans as they can,
no matter who it is, they're all agreed,
every child, every woman, every man.
For human life is precious and unique,
without the NHS life would be bleak.

In Memoriam

I watched as little robin hopped about
then vainly flew towards the jasmine bush
a hawk swooped down with such a deadly clout
and fearsome talons grabbed in such a rush.
The hungry bird thus landed on the ground
and stared at me so haughty and assured,
its luckless prey lay still without a sound,
by vicious claws entrapped and well secured.
Then it flew off with quarry to consume,
in some lone shadey place and out of sight,
no peaceful death, no hallowed silent tomb
its end was quick, no time for any fright.
I'd stood and witnessed killing quite in awe,
as surely nature's *"red in tooth and claw."

* Alfred, Lord Tennyson. In memoriam AHH 1849

Seasons have their Day

The days get shorter as the winter creeps
from northern skies and brings the colder air.
The trees are naked and now gently sleep
but quietly waiting, still, and standing there.
As silently first snows came down last night
just like a blanket covering the ground.
It filled the woodland scene with dazzling light
as morning sunshine glitters all around.
The silence is intense and nothing stirs
the bitter cold has muffled everything.
No life is here as every migrant bird
has flown away and will return in Spring.
The seasons roll around so we take stock
and mark the time just like a ticking clock.

Sunrise in the Woods

The darkness of the woods seems to ignite
as sun pours down across the canopy.
As fading shadows waken from the night
with sparkling jewels of royal panoply.
The molten puddles scatter on the ground,
as if the crucible had broken trust.
With darkling velvet lying all around
that once were fallen leaves but now are dust.
The mystery of the fiery sun above
which warms our earth and gives us every day
has covered us with warmth and heavenly love
and through the leaves will always finds its way.
When darkness is dispelled by brightest light
like truth, it always will the liar fright!

On Listening to the Song of a Robin

Each morning brings sweet songs from up above
within the tangle of the leafless tree.
What is this song, these joyful sounds of love,
which wrap the frosty air in harmony?
This singer hides so shy and yet so bold.
His whistling tunes evoke another dream,
a natural place of peace and not so cold,
with summer sun and shaded sparkling stream.
At first I cannot see through all the wood,
he's hard to spot but then a flash of red,
revealed his hiding place and there he stood.
Gave me a look and then he sadly fled.
The moment we enjoy his cheerful song
is such a special thing yet lasts not long.

Our Garden

Our garden is a sanctuary for us,
a place in which to rest and entertain.
The care of it, a labour without fuss,
on sunny days or even in the rain.
The dahlia and the daisy are all here,
the rooted cuttings and the older plants,
it all appears and changes year to year
and some things just arrive by lucky chance.
The snowdrops and the daffodils are first
and then the tulips flaunt their gorgeous heads.
Soon it is time to slake our yearning thirst
for shades and tints in crowded flower beds.
And don't forget the frogs, the birds, the bees
they have much work to do, no time for ease!

The Ancient Tree

The ancient tree has stood there for an age,
a silent witness to our foolish ways.
It's seen the fires of hopelessness and rage,
which wrought our conflicts during many days.
At times the sun did shine and skies were blue,
and love and laughter filled the pretty glades.
The people frolicked there with nought to do
or made a picnic in its dappled shades.
Now we are living in a time of fear,
for we have burnt too much and CO_2
increases now with every year on year.
We wring our hands and know what we should do,
and if we fail to put this matter right
well, we will have just one eternal night!

Victoria Plums

We have just had our first good crop of plums,
until this year we've never seen the fruit.
In spring the gorgeous blossom came up trumps,
and now we've feasted well, on all its loot.
Plum tarts were made and much enjoyed by all,
the glorious fruit so ruby rich and fine.
The sweetest taste which never seems to pall
has made us smile and tasted so divine.
But all too soon the tree has no more plums,
with fruit all gone and nothing left but leaves.
We now await the wintry blast which comes
and long for spring when warmer air relieves.
For seasons come and go as well they must
and future harvests will provide, we trust.

Mountains of the Western Isles

Those distant mountains seem to beckon me
their mighty strength lies hidden as they sleep.
When gazing at them from across the sea
my feelings for them go so very deep.
What power resides within their massive shapes?
What hold has it upon my heart and soul?
When wrapped in cloud these ancient landscapes,
which primal folk just wanted to extol
along the coastline of the Western Isles.
So many places have a tale to tell
of battles and of hardship and exiles
and fateful journeys battered in the swell.
For we are fragile creatures, not of stone
but in these places we are not alone.

The Joy of Snow

A single, silent flake of snow flew by,
for us to watch across the window pane.
It flew just like a feather from the sky
'twas shed when swans flew high up in a skein.
Soon more and more snow laid upon the ground
which made a muffling layer of purest white,
the sparkling sky was swirling all around,
The day was bathed in such a wintry light.
We welcomed such a change of snowy scene,
and danced our footprints out across the lawn,
but soon the snow was melting down a stream,
the fun had gone and all was now forlorn.
For joy of snow will promise magic days
but really causes nothing but delays.

A Merry Dance

We came into this world without a care,
our parents met by random chance alone.
We are as spirits conjured from the air,
yet we are made of sinew, flesh and bone.
We have no say in what our kind will be,
and cannot chose the colour of our skin.
We have no way our future to foresee,
and never know what place we'll finish in.
We all just want a happy life and peace,
to share a world of harmony and love.
From war and hate will we not get release,
by sending olive branch on wings of dove?
Well, all our life is just a merry dance,
we've some control, but mostly it's all chance.

Byng Brook Bomb-Hole

In Ufford there's a special place to swim,
the Byng Brook flows, beside a winding lane,
a quiet place where water hoppers skim.
formed when Nazi bombers dropped their "rain"
But now it is a place of peace and calm,
where cattle come to drink and chew the cud,
They're safe from bombs and wander from the farm
to stand and stare, up to their knees in mud.
Not many people bathe here but a few,
to wallow in the pool on sunny day,
in fact there's only one or maybe two,
and sometimes children who just want to play.
Byng Brook meanders on to greater things,
then joins the Deben as do several springs.

Sleepless in Melton

I woke at ten to three again today,
my head was filled with many scarey thoughts,
I worried for this world in disarray,
and restless, felt completely out of sorts.
We humans have made such a mess of it.
The virus still destroys our crazy world,
everything is turning now to s…t,
into the void all our stuff is hurled.
So I got up to make a cup of tea,
to write these lines and set my mind at ease.
To try to come to terms with what I see.
And not to fret about some vile disease.
For us the future's not so very clear,
It's sink or swim our only choice I fear.

Owning a Boat

A long dark winter is the time to scrape
the barnacles and rust that undermine.
Then paint it red with anti-foul and tape
to keep it neat along the plimsoll line.
Now sand down all the wood and check for leaks.
We'll varnish where we've rubbed and paint the rails,
next, oil the hinge to stop annoying squeaks,
carefully fold away the precious sails.
Dreaming of far off summer days of sun,
to drift with tides and anchor where we will,
that is the prize when all this work is done,
a life afloat and all it can fulfill.
We are an island race it's in our blood,
and know to stay away from banks of mud.